Story Starters

Animal Creatures

Name _____

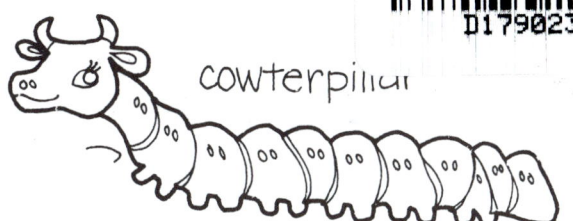

Use the facts you have just completed and finish this story that is started for you.

Not many people know the true story of how the _____
_{name of animal}

became a combination of a/an _____ and a/an _____.

Many years ago in the tropical jungle of Kora-Kora there lived a wizard who had all kinds of magical powers. He was a happy, kind wizard, but he had a terrible memory and could never remember anything from one minute to the next.

One day _____

_____

_____

_____

_____

_____

(Finish your story on the back of this paper.)

Creative Writing Roundup
© 1976 — The Learning Works, Inc.

Story Starters   Name _____

The Wacky Invention

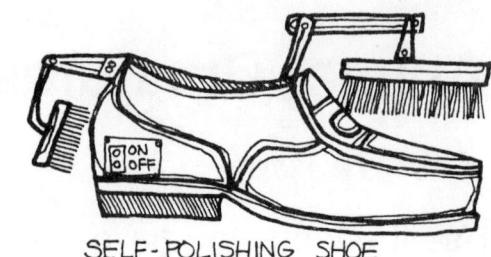
SELF-POLISHING SHOE

Write the answers to these statements.

1. I have just completed a new invention called a _____.

2. This invention makes my life easier by _____
   _____.

3. I got the bright idea for my invention when _____
   _____.

4. This is how my invention actually works _____
   _____
   _____.

5. When I took my invention to school, my friends _____
   _____.

6. My mom and dad think _____
   _____.

7. This is what my invention looks like.

The Secret Formula

Use the facts you have completed on the opposite page and finish this story that is already started for you.

    My strange discovery of the secret formula came quite by accident. It all happened the day I dropped the bottle containing the mysterious liquid. Then right before my eyes

_____

_____

_____

_____

_____

_____

(Finish your story on the back of this paper.)

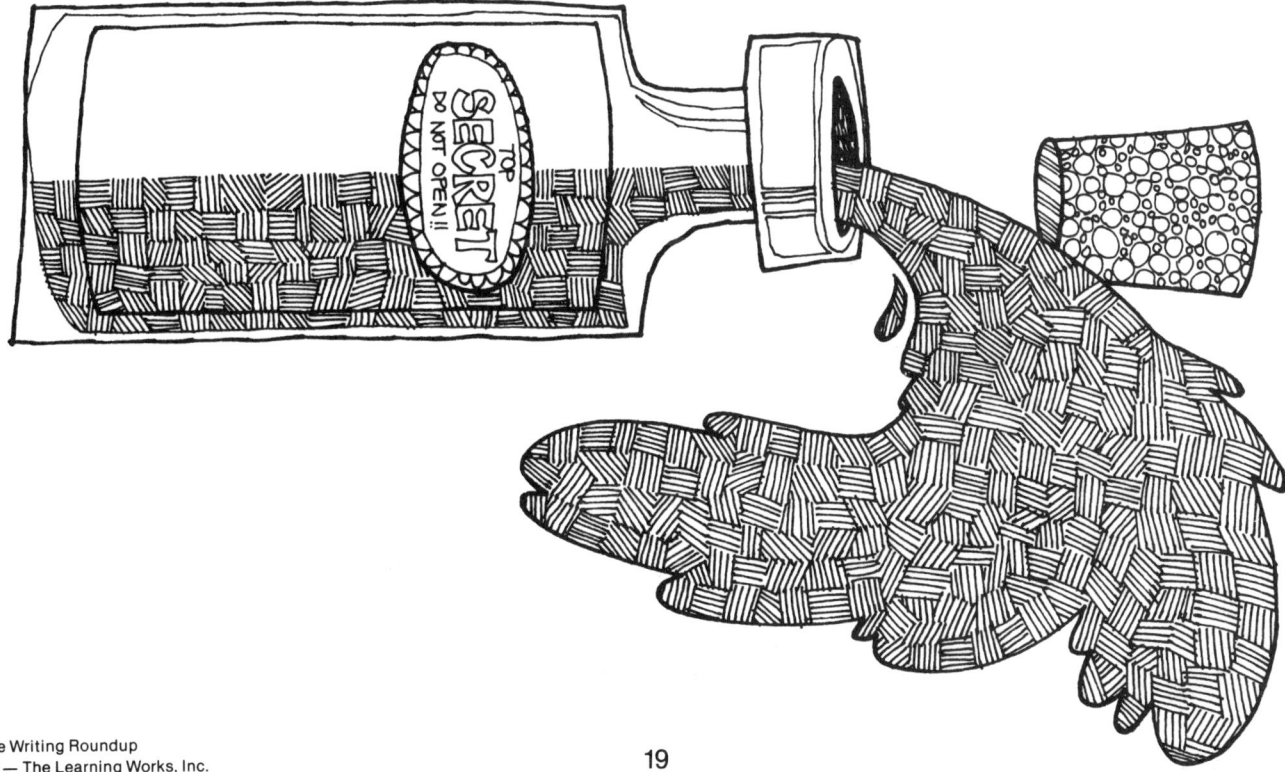

Brainstorming a Theme

Name _____

Brainstorm a Pirate

1. Think about the word PIRATE. What words do you think of when you see the word PIRATE?

2. Some words are written for you in the pirate's hat below. Can you add several words to this list?

3. Use the words in the pirate's hat and write a short story. The story is started to get you on your way.

He was a mean-looking pirate. He had a black eye patch over his left eye, and he wore a hat with a picture of skull and crossbones.

_____

_____

_____

_____

_____

(Finish your story on the back of this paper.)

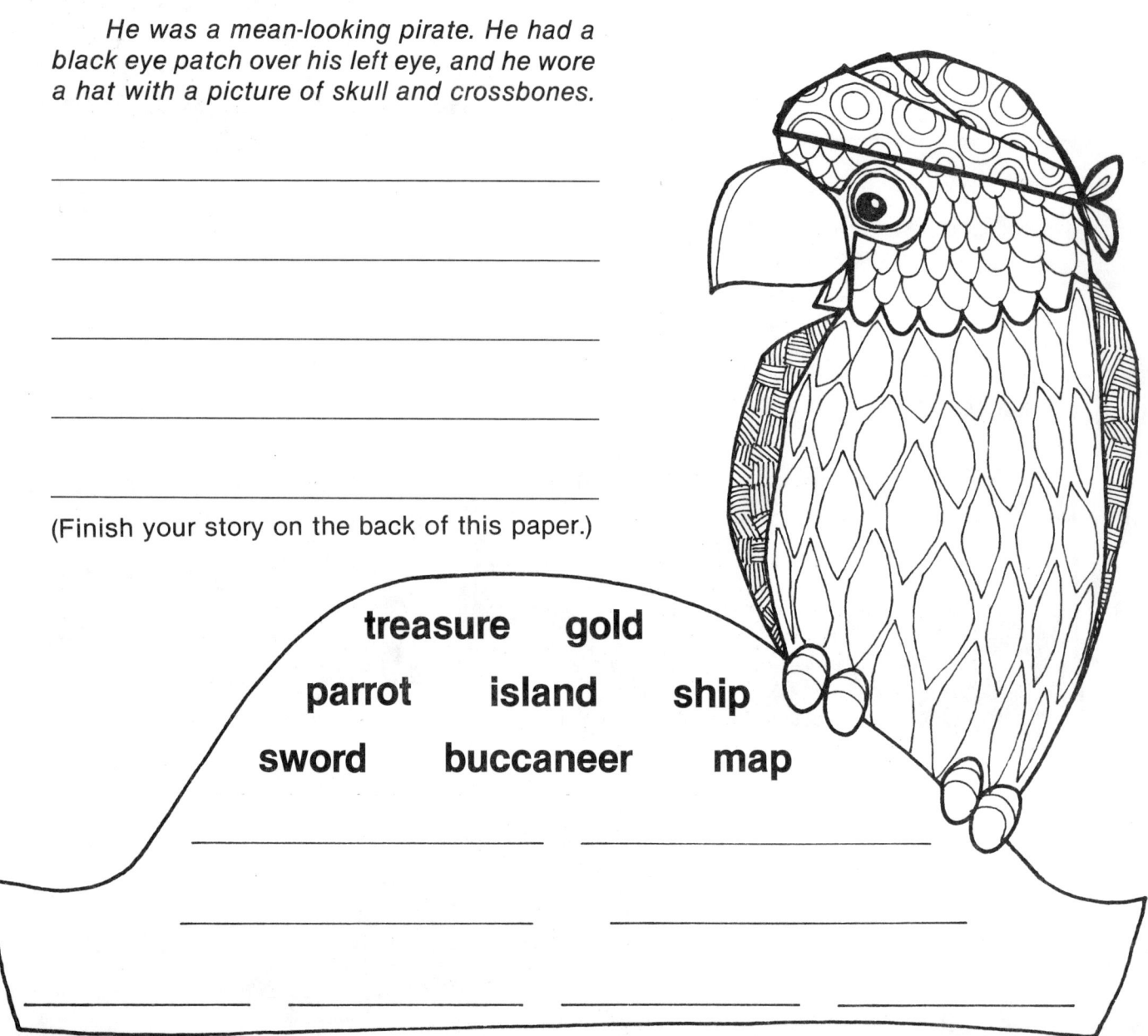

treasure   gold
parrot   island   ship
sword   buccaneer   map

The Learning Works

P.O. Box 6187 Santa Barbara, CA 93160

The purchase of this book entitles the
individual teacher to reproduce copies for use
in the classroom.

The reproduction of any part for an entire
school or school system or for commercial
use is strictly prohibited.

No form of this work may be reproduced
or transmitted or recorded without written
permission from the publisher.

Copyright © 1976 – THE LEARNING WORKS
All rights reserved.
Printed in the United States of America.

THE CREATIVE WRITING ROUNDUP.

Copyright © 1976 – THE LEARNING WORKS

TABLE OF CONTENTS

Part One — Story Starters

Animal Creatures 6-7

The Wacky Invention 8-9

Principal for the Day 10-11

The Capturing of a Glurble 12-13

The Super Sundae 14-15

The Flying Tennis Shoes 16-17

The Secret Formula 18-19

Part Two — Brainstorming a Theme

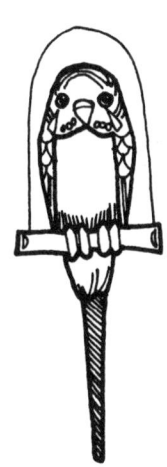

Brainstorm a Pirate 20

Brainstorm Boot 21

Monster Brainstorm 22

Doctor Brainstorm 23

Brainstorm a Pet 24

Bubble Gum Brainstorm 25

Brainstorm a Rocket 26

Brainstorm a Hippopotamus 27

Part Three — Motivators

Prefix Pet	28
Fun Foursomes	29
Proverb Puzzler	30
Alphabet Happenings	31
The Hole Story	32
The Night the Power Pooped Out	33
Franny Farmer's Secret	34
Alphabet Animal Story	35

Part Four — Poetry

Put Yourself in a Poem	36
What Fun to See	37
Animal Poems	38
Color Rhymes	39
Simile Poems	40
Riddle Riot	41
Expressing Your Emotions	42

cozy as a sleeping bag

Part Five — Learning Center Writing Ideas

General Story Ideas	43
Just for Fun	44
Animal Stories	45
Adventure	46
Mystery	47
Sports	48

Brainstorm Boot

1. Think about the word BOOT. What words do you think of when you see the word BOOT?

2. Write eight or more words in the boot below.

3. Use your list of related words and write a short story. Give your story an interesting title.

(Finish your story on the back of this paper.)

Brainstorming a Theme Name _____

Monster Brainstorm

1. Write eight or more words you can think of when you see the word MONSTER.
2. Use the words you have listed in the monster and write a short story.

_____

_____

_____

_____

_____

(Finish your story on the back of this paper.)

Brainstorming a Theme

Name _____

Doctor Brainstorm

1. Write down eight or more words you think of when you see the word DOCTOR.

2. Use the words you have listed and write a short story below.

_____

_____

_____

_____

(Finish your story on the back of this paper.)

Brainstorm a Pet

1. Write eight or more words you think of when you see the word PET.
2. Use these words and write a short story about a pet.

(Finish your story on the back of this paper.)

Brainstorming a Theme   Name _____

Bubble Gum Brainstorm

1. Write down eight or more words you think of when you see the words BUBBLE GUM.
2. Use the words you have listed inside the bubble gum and write a short story.

_____
_____
_____
_____
_____

(Finish your story on the back of this paper.)

Brainstorm a Rocket

1. Write down eight or more words you think of when you see the word ROCKET.

2. Use the words you have listed inside the rocket and write a short story.

_____

_____

_____

_____

_____

_____

_____

(Finish your story on the back of this paper.)

Name _____

Brainstorm a Hippopotamus

1. Write down eight or more words you think of when you see the word HIPPOPOTAMUS.

2. Use the words you have listed inside the hippo and write a short story.

(Finish your story on the back of this paper.)

Prefix Pet

1. Create a PREFIX PET by combining words and prefixes.
2. Use some of the prefixes listed below or come up with your own.

   Example: a tri-bellied, uni-headed, bi-footed polygurgle.

Some common prefixes:

uni - one	hex - six	ped - foot
bi - two	sept - seven	hyper - over
tri - three	octa - eight	sub - under
quad - four	deca - ten	
quint - five	poly - many	

Suggested words to use:

toed	headed
footed	fingered
eyed	nosed
tailed	eared
bellied	horned

BI-HEADED
HYPERACTIVE
SCALY-TAILED
OCTAHORN

3. Draw a picture of your PREFIX PET.

Motivators

Name _____

Fun Foursomes

1. Choose **one** of the groups of words below.
2. Write a story and use each of the four words in the group you chose.
3. Underline each of the four words as you use it in your story.
4. Check to see that your story has a good beginning, middle, and end.

monkey	sheriff	banana
pickle	penny	telephone
bubble gum	balloon	ice cube
clock	adhesive strip	owl

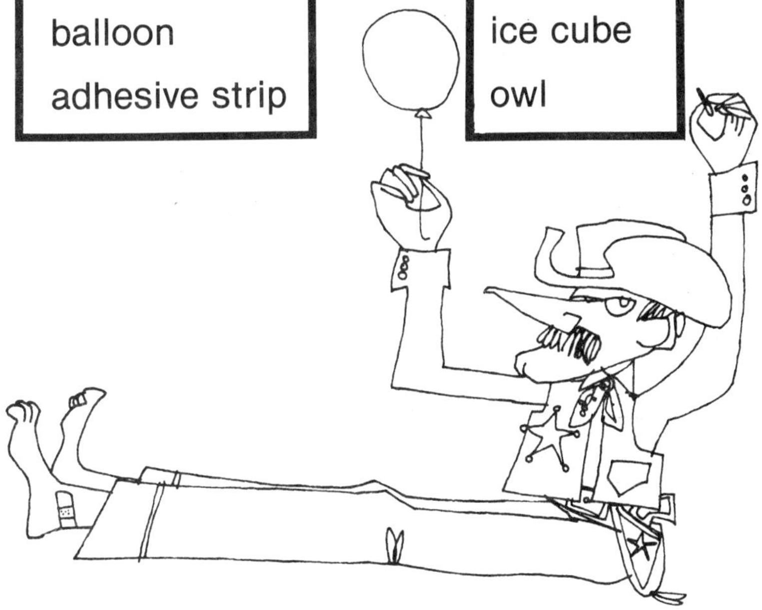

(Finish your story on the back of this paper.)

Creative Writing Roundup
© 1976 — The Learning Works, Inc.

Motivators   Name _____

Proverb Puzzler

1. Pick a famous proverb from the list below, or choose one of your own.

2. Change as many of the words as you can so that it means the same thing, but sounds very different.

3. Use a dictionary or thesaurus to help you find synonyms or words that mean the same thing.

   Example: "An overabundance of chefs ruins the chicken soup."

   (Too many cooks spoil the broth.)

Proverbs:
An apple a day keeps the doctor away.
A stitch in time saves nine.
Look before you leap.
In one ear and out the other.
A bird in the hand is worth two in the bush.
Don't count your chickens before they hatch.
A rolling stone gathers no moss.
There is not fire without some smoke.
Don't cry over spilled milk.

4. Write your PROVERB PUZZLER here. Illustrate your proverb.

Alphabet Happenings

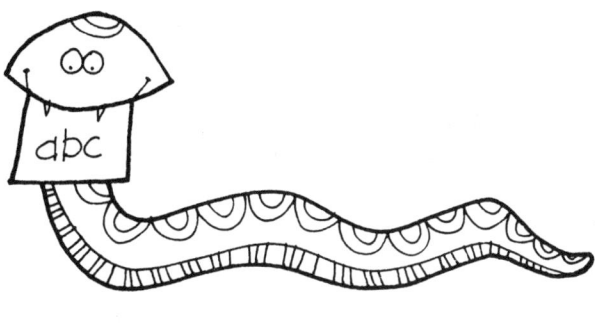

1. Pick a letter of the alphabet.
2. Draw a large picture of your letter below.
3. Write a description and begin each line with the letter you chose.

Example:

Snakes
lip
lowly
ilently through
wamps.

The Hole Story

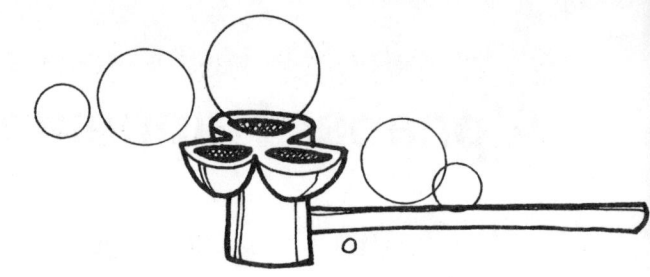

1. Make a list of ten things that have some type of hole. Examples: scissors, a salt shaker, a drinking straw.

2. Pick any three of the objects from your list to write about.

3. On a piece of white art paper, draw a picture of one of your objects and actually cut out the hole. Color your picture.

4. Write a paragraph describing your object. Pretend you are describing it to a person who has never seen this object before. Tell what this object is used for, tell about its size and shape, and what it is made of.

5. Make a picture and write a paragraph for each of your three objects. Do each one on a separate sheet of paper. Display your finished HOLE STORIES for others to enjoy.

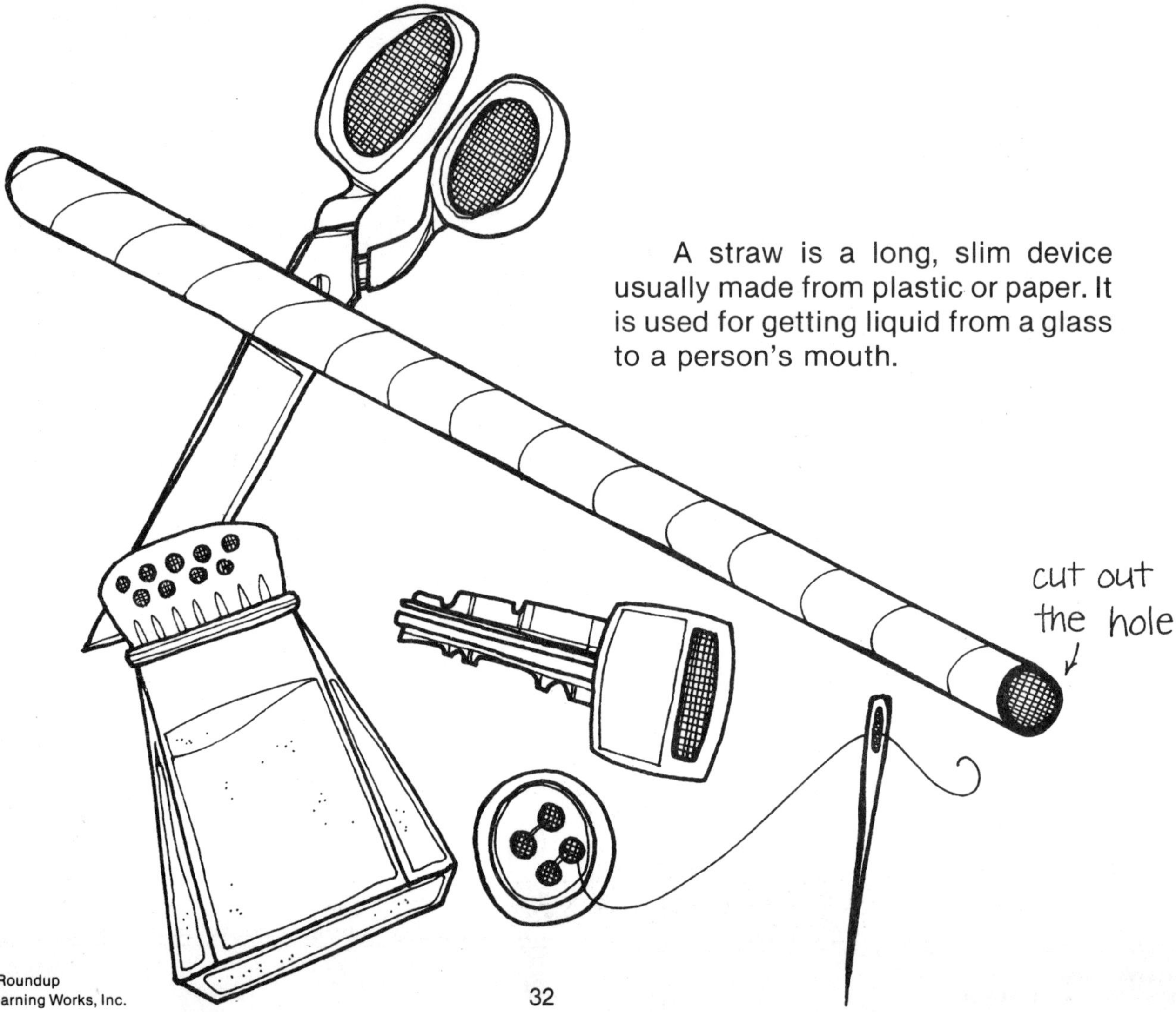

A straw is a long, slim device usually made from plastic or paper. It is used for getting liquid from a glass to a person's mouth.

cut out the hole

The Night the Power Pooped Out

What would happen if all electrical power in the entire world stopped for twenty four hours?

On a piece of scratch paper, list things that would no longer work without electricity. (Examples: televisions would go off, elevators would stop, and refrigerators would not operate.)

Use your list and write a story about where you were and what happened to you. . . . .

The Night the Power Pooped Out

_____

_____

_____

_____

_____

_____

_____

_____

_____

_____

_____

_____

(Finish your story on the back of this paper.)

Franny Farmer's Secret

Franny Farmer wanted to plant tomato seeds, but ended up with magical seeds instead. Only you and Franny know the wonderful powers of those magical seeds. Now you are about to tell the whole story.

In your story, answer the following questions.

1. What do the seeds look like?
2. Where did Franny plant them?
3. What are the special powers of the seeds?
4. What kind of trouble do the seeds get Franny Farmer into?
5. What do the neighbors say about the seeds?
6. What finally happens to Franny and her seeds?

_____

_____

_____

_____

_____

_____

_____

_____

(Finish your story on the back of this paper.)

Alphabet Animal Story

1. Cut out about fifteen letters of different shapes, sizes, and colors from a magazine.

2. Arrange your letters in the shape of a make-believe animal like the one shown at the right.

3. Paste your animal in the cage below.

4. Write a story about your ALPHABET ANIMAL.

5. Start many of the words with the same letter of the alphabet.

Example: George the giraffe grew up in Georgia. He was a great golfer but was not a very good gourd grower. Most of the time he was gracious, generous, and gentle, but sometimes he grew grumpy and greedy.

GENUINE ALPHA-BEAST
DON'T FEED THE ANIMALS

(Finish your story on the back of this paper.)

Put Yourself in a Poem

1. Write your name in capital letters going down the paper.

2. Use each letter of your name to begin a line of your poem.

3. Each line should tell about YOU. For example, tell about your likes and dislikes. It does not have to rhyme.

Example:

LISA
Loves to climb trees.
Interested in books about horses.
Someday wants to be a doctor.
Always laughing and talking.

Poetry

What Fun to See

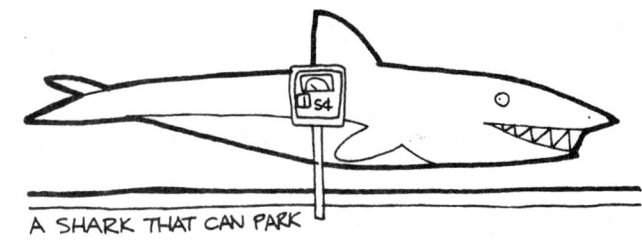
A SHARK THAT CAN PARK

1. Fill in the blanks with two rhyming words:

   What fun to see a _____ that can _____!

   Examples: What fun to see a **pie** that can **fly**!
   What fun to see a **hog** that can **jog**!

2. Write four "what fun to see" rhymes using the lines below.

3. Then pick your best rhyme and illustrate it below.

_____

_____

_____

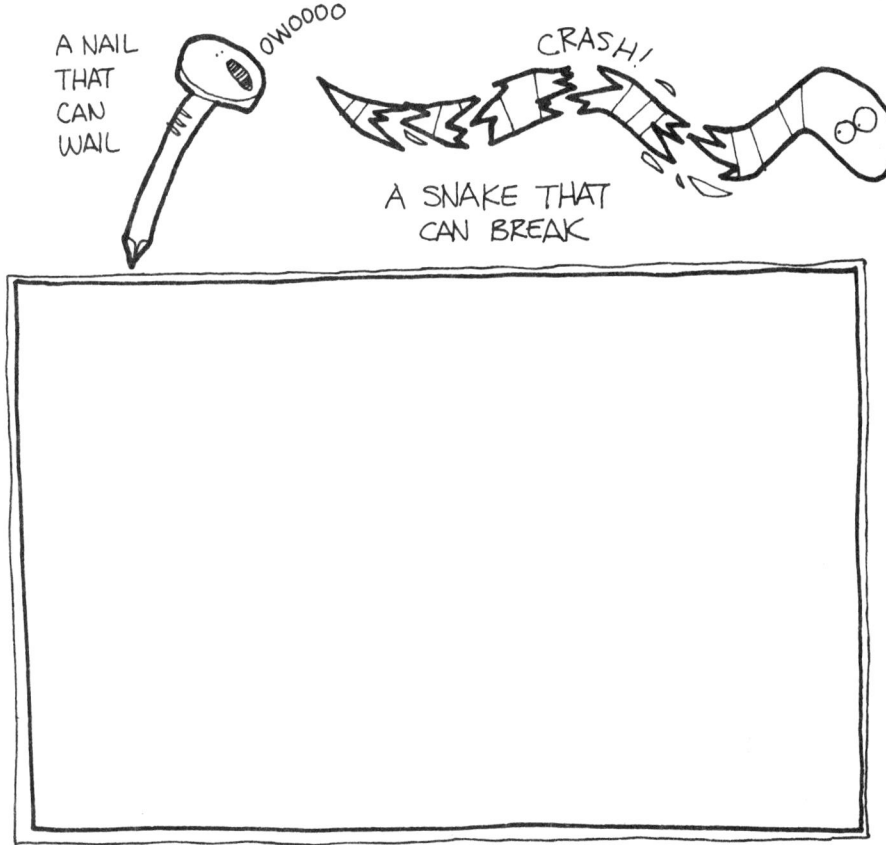
A NAIL THAT CAN WAIL

A SNAKE THAT CAN BREAK

ILLUSTRATE YOUR RHYME HERE

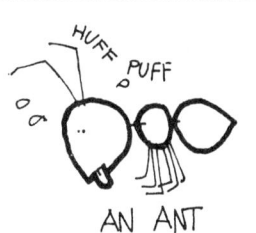
AN ANT THAT CAN PANT

A LOCK THAT CAN KNOCK

A NUT THAT CAN PUTT

Creative Writing Roundup
© 1976 — The Learning Works, Inc.

Poetry   Name _____

Animal Poems

1. Pick an animal that you would like to write about.

2. Study this sample and notice how many words are on each line.

MONKEY	(one word)
LONG TAIL	(two words)
SOFT, BROWN FUR	(three words)
SWINGING FROM A TREE	(four words)
IN THE JUNGLE,	(three words)
LOOKING SO	(two words)
CAREFREE.	(one word)

3. Do you see the pattern?

4. Now fill in the missing lines. Make sure you have the right number of words.

ALLIGATOR
CRAWLING REPTILE

_____

_____

_____

IN THE
SWAMP.

5. Use this pattern and write your own animal poem.

_____

_____

_____

_____

_____

_____

_____

Creative Writing Roundup
© 1976 — The Learning Works, Inc.   38

Color Rhymes

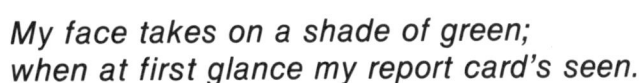

1. Choose a favorite color, and write a poem of two lines.
2. Both lines should end in rhyming words.

Example:

*My father's face is the color red;
when it's way past time I should be in bed.*

*My face takes on a shade of green;
when at first glance my report card's seen.*

Finish these poems:

The color yellow is like the sun;

_____

Black is like the evening sky;

_____

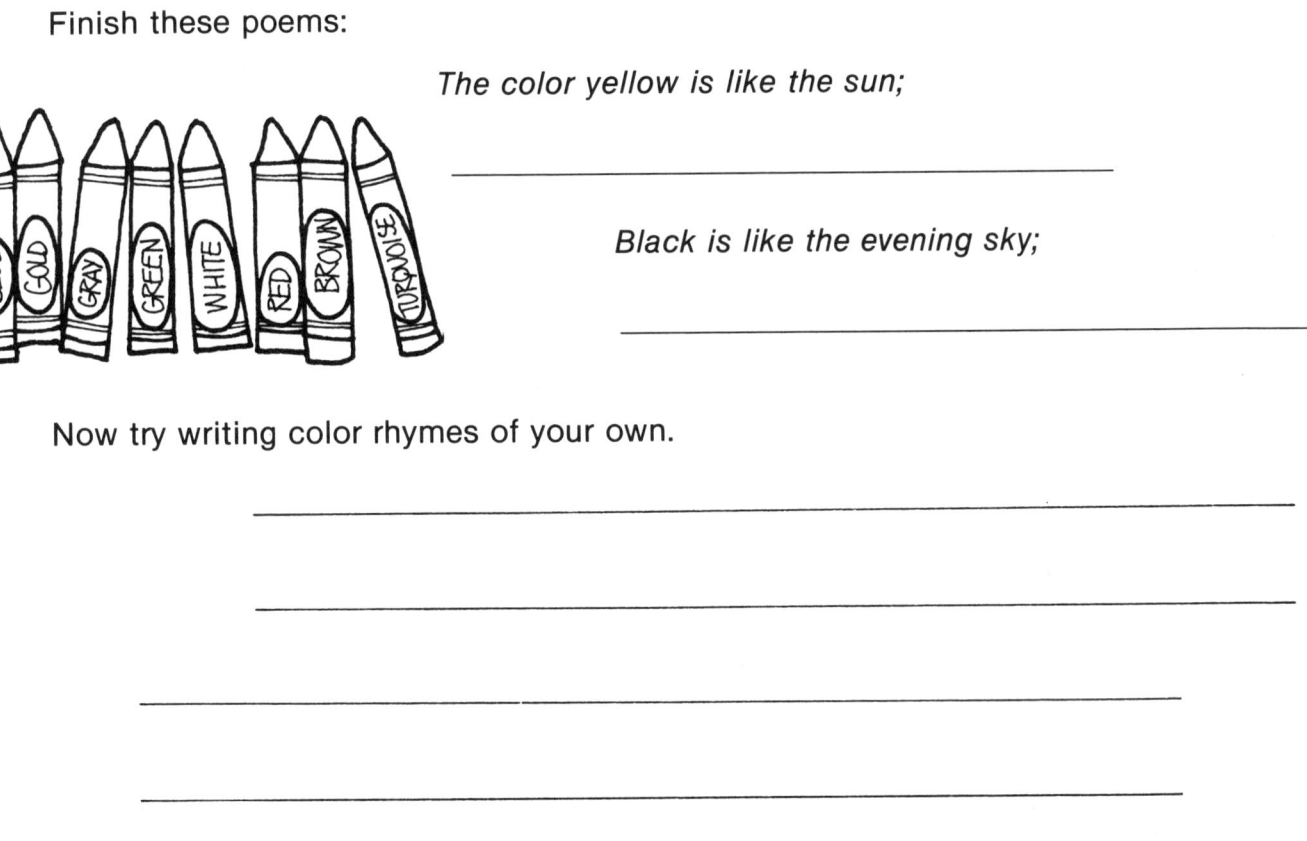

Now try writing color rhymes of your own.

_____

_____

_____

_____

_____

Poetry

Name _____

Simile Poems

1. A simile is when you compare two things using the words "like" or "as."

    Example: Yellow is **like** the happiness inside me.

    The snow is as soft **as** a whisper.

2. Write a poem and use the words LIKE or AS on each line. (Your poem does not have to rhyme).

    Example: The color black is as dark **as** the middle of the night.

    Black smells **like** air that is filled with smog.

    Black is **like** my mood when it is raining, and I want to play outside.

    Black is **like** my feet going barefoot through the mud.

3. Now write a simile poem. You might want to use your five senses in comparing things (smell, feel, sight, sound, and taste).

    _____

    _____

    _____

    _____

    _____

    _____

Creative Writing Roundup
© 1976 — The Learning Works, Inc.

Riddle Riot

 I'm tiny. I'm brown. I ride around town
In the fur of a cat, or a dog or rat.

1. Write a riddle about something you see or use every day.
2. Make lines one and two rhyme; lines three and four rhyme.

Example: Although I'm not part of the human **race**,

I have two hands and a big round **face**.

I'm sometimes seen hanging on a **wall**,

I've got lots of numbers but am not too **tall**.

What am I?

Did you guess a clock? Right. Now fill in the missing lines of this riddle and make it rhyme.

You can find me shining in the sky,

_____

I give you light and lots of heat,

_____

Now write your own RIDDLE RIOT. Give your riddle to a classmate and see if he or she can guess what you wrote about.

_____

_____

_____

_____

Try another RIDDLE RIOT on the back of this paper.   WHAT AM I?

I have two eyes, I have a tail.
In Gold Rush days I carried mail.
I have a mane, I have some hoofs,
I hardly ever sleep on roofs.

Expressing Your Emotions

1. Write a poem of two or more lines about your feelings.

2. The first and second lines should rhyme; the third and fourth lines should rhyme.

   Examples: *I feel as lonely as can be,*
   Since my best friend moved away from me.

   or

   I feel so angry and full of gloom,
   When my little brother sneaks in my room.
   He makes me angry as can be,
   He does not respect my privacy.

3. Here are some emotions you might want to write a poem about...

fear	happiness	jealousy
love	excitement	loneliness
joy	sadness	anger

_____

_____

_____

_____

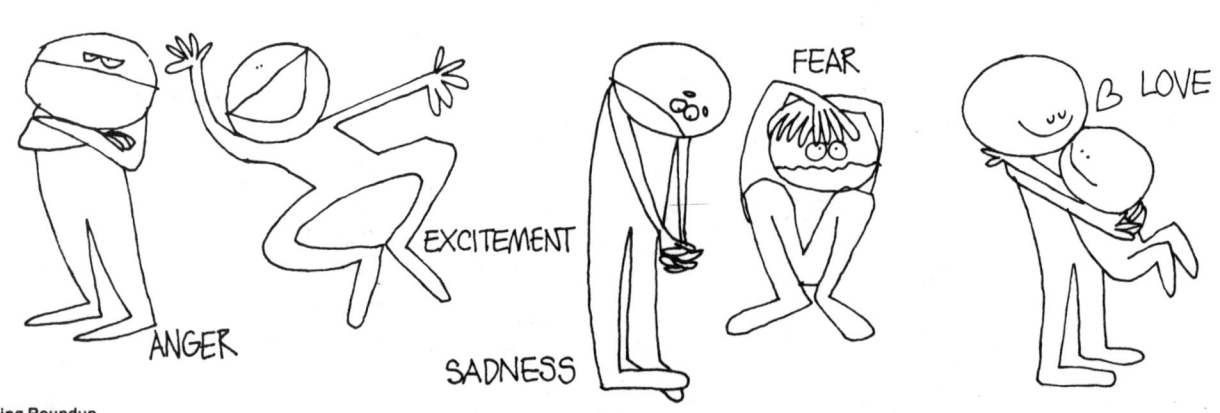

General Story Ideas

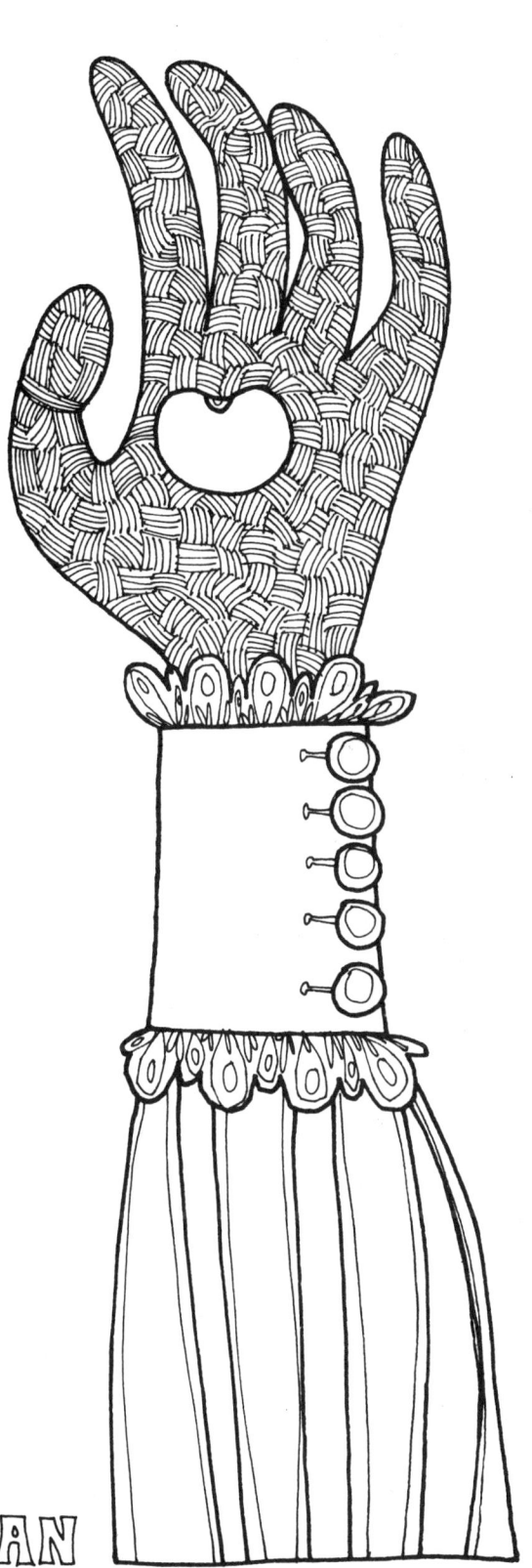

1. The Polka-Dotted Package
2. A Dream Come True
3. The Runaway
4. The Magic Lima Bean
5. Friends to the End
6. The Toothpaste King
7. Nobody Notices
8. The Day My Face Turned Red
9. New to the School
10. Try, Try Again
11. Once Too Often
12. My Turn To Shine
13. That's What Friends Are For
14. The Moment of Truth
15. I'll Never Forget
16. The Playground Secret
17. The Best Day of My Life
18. The Big Move
19. Not a Moment Too Soon
20. The Most Important Decision

THE MAGIC LIMA BEAN

Just For Fun

1. Little Lucy's Lollipop
2. Dorinda, the Door
3. What I Love Best About the Bo Tiddle
4. Bubble Trouble
5. Super Spy for the F.B.I.
6. The Nervous Noodle
7. The Popcorn Popper That Wouldn't Stop Popping
8. The T.V. That Talked Back
9. The Skunk That Joined the Team
10. The Day it Rained Chocolate Drops
11. The Shoes That Could Fly
12. When the Numbers Disappeared
13. The Grimble Who Lost His Frisbee
14. The Dipsy Doodle
15. The Girl Who Couldn't Stop Giggling
16. If I Had Four Eyes
17. When the Flowers Could Sing
18. The Apple That Grew on the Orange Tree
19. Backwards Day
20. Mr. Killybopper's Bad Mistake

Animal Stories

1. The Bashful Porcupine
2. The Camel Comedy
3. The Skunk That Loved Bubble Gum
4. The Horse That Joined the Circus
5. The Flea That Could Sing
6. A Cat in Trouble
7. Moose on the Loose
8. My Pet, the T.V. Star
9. A Monkey Named Mumbles
10. The Ten-Armed Octopus
11. The Caterpillar That Roared
12. My Pet is Missing
13. Six Cats Too Many
14. The Elephant That Never Laughed
15. The Fish That Watched T.V.
16. The Empty Cage
17. The Day of the Pet Contest
18. Willie, the Worm
19. The Rattlesnake That Lost his Rattle
20. Molly Mae, the Mouse

MOOSE ON THE LOOSE

Adventure

1. Adrift on a Raft
2. The Day the Earth Shook
3. To Climb the Mountain
4. Caught in the Storm
5. Journey by Balloon
6. I Was a Stowaway
7. Adventure Beneath the Sea
8. The Runaway Motorcycle
9. Race the Rapids
10. The Storm at Sea
11. Alone and Lost
12. The Race Against Time
13. My Life as a Skydiver
14. Adventures on an African Safari
15. Caught in Quicksand
16. Astronauts in Trouble
17. A Long Day's Journey
18. Survival
19. No Way Out
20. Caught in a Hurricane

Mystery

1. Mystery of the Missing Mummy
2. The Disappearing Wall
3. Clue of the Claws
4. Strange Sound at the Window
5. The Creature of the Night
6. Sloop, the Spy
7. Ghosts' Night Out
8. The Creeping Shadow
9. The Vanishing Bicycle
10. The Case of the Golden Key
11. Danger From Within
12. No Warning
13. Three Clues to Trouble
14. The Writing on the Wall
15. A Cry in the Night
16. The Message in the Bottle
17. The Revenge of the Rodents
18. The Creak of the Door
19. The Case of the Stolen Wallet
20. How Detective Donahue Solved the Dippenger Mystery

Name _____

Sports

1. The Wringers vs. the Stingers
2. The Daring Diver
3. Conquer the Waves
4. That Championship Game
5. Frieda, of Football Fame
6. Last on the Team
7. Football Hero
8. The Story of Benny the Baseball Kid
9. Vacation at Ski Village
10. My Life as a Catcher's Mitt
11. Newcomer to the Squad
12. The Tennis Ball That Lost Its Bounce
13. Ringside with Max, the Muscle
14. Bernie, the Baseball Bumbler
15. Touchdown in Time
16. Race Against the Clock
17. What It's Like to be a Basketball Net
18. The Hockey Happening
19. An Athlete's Dream Come True
20. The Play That Changed the Game

FRIEDA OF FOOTBALL FAME